Original title:

The Snowman's Melting Heart

Author: Olivia Sterling

ISBN HARDBACK: 978-9916-94-394-6

ISBN PAPERBACK: 978-9916-94-395-3

A Toneless Goodbye

With winter's chill, joy took its flight,
A jolly figure lost to the night.
He waved his arms, so wide and grand,
But 'no solid plans' was his last stand.

The sun peeked in with a cheeky grin,
His carrot nose began to thin.
With every chuckle, a puddle grew,
"I'm just a splash now, who knew?" he blew.

Mittens and scarf, now in a heap,
"I'm melting faster than I can leap!"
He tiptoed lightly, feeling so spry,
Dropping his buttons with a sigh.

So long dear friends, I've lost my snow,
I'm off to dance where the warm winds blow.
Laughing all the way, what a sight to see,
As a pint-sized puddle, I'll still be me!

Gleaming Horizons

In a world of white, he found his cheer,
With frosty bits that spun near and dear.
His eyes made of coal, so bright and wide,
Chasing the sun was his favorite ride.

The warmth of spring with a wink and nod,
His belly, once round, now felt a bit odd.
As he danced with joy, his edges grew thin,
"Just a little more sun, and let the fun begin!"

Snowflakes fell like ticker-tape streams,
He twirled like a star, lost in daydreams.
With each silly shimmy, a drip-drip sound,
The snowmen laughed at the joy all around.

So here's to the glow of horizons so bright,
Even as temperature takes a bite.
With a twinkle and giggle, he stepped aside,
Towards a fate where laughter would slide!

Where Frost Meets Flame

In a world where frost does dance,
Warmth arrives with a silly prance.
A carrot nose begins to sway,
As sunshine laughs and steals the day.

With boots that squeak and mittens too,
Melting limbs feel the sun's debut.
He grins with glee, a puddly mess,
Yet claims it's merely summer's dress.

The Ebb of Winter

Winter's grin is fading fast,
As puddles gather on the grass.
His frosty limbs begin to drip,
He hiccups, oh, what a funny slip!

Each drop a giggle, what a sight,
As snowflakes twirl in morning light.
A frozen chap with a sunny face,
Slips and twirls in a melting race.

Echoes of a Melting Soul

Beneath the sun, a snowman sighs,
Complaining just beneath blue skies.
With every ray, he giggles loud,
His icy ego can't be proud.

He tries to dance but soon he slips,
His frosty feet are ready to quit.
A funny jig, he drips and sways,
A slip, a flop, in sunlit ways.

Beneath a Shimmering Veil

Hidden under glimmers bright,
A chilly heart takes to flight.
But warmth is here, a cheeky tease,
As melting snow becomes a breeze.

With every puddle, a laugh erupts,
A frosty fellow who simply fluffs.
"Is this a sauna?" he asks in glee,
Dancing freely, a sight to see.

Bits of White and Warmth

In the yard a frosty friend,
With a carrot nose, he'd pretend.
But as the sun begins to grin,
He loses bits of joy within.

His hat slides down, his scarf does droop,
He's quite the soggy, floppy troop.
His laughter bubbles, melts away,
As puddles start to save the day!

When Spirits Melt

With each sunbeam, he starts to shake,
A giggle here, a splish-splash break.
His friends all cheer, 'You're doing great!'
But puddles form at quite a rate.

A drip, a drop, oh what a sight,
Our buddy slips, oh what a fright!
He twirls around, his joy runs free,
A dancing blob of icy glee!

The Pulse of Thawing

From solid crust to merry stream,
He quakes and quips, quite the dream.
His arms are flailing, legs a-shake,
A wobbly jig, make no mistake!

He once was proud, now he's a drip,
Yet still he waves, won't lose his grip.
A splash of joy, oh what a thrill,
A frosty frolic, a cheerful chill!

Dichotomy of Ice and Fire

The sun's warm kiss, a playful tease,
He sways and shivers in the breeze.
'I'm fine!', he yells, but starts to fade,
A wobbly hero, unafraid.

With each warm laugh, he splats and glides,
In every drop, his spirit hides.
A blend of cold and warmth so bright,
A frozen friend in sheer delight!

A Heart's Softening

In a frosty park, he stood so proud,
With a carrot nose, he laughed out loud.
But a sunbeam grinned, oh what a tease,
He wobbled and wiggled, melting with ease.

His coal eyes twinkled, a sight to see,
As puddles formed, he squeaked with glee.
"Chill out!" he shouted to the warm, bright day,
"I'll slide into spring and dance my way!"

The Last Embrace of Winter

Winter's grip is loosening now,
But the snowman just won't take a bow.
He chuckled and slipped on his icy spot,
"If I'm going down, I'll make it hot!"

With every thaw, his cheeks turned pink,
He waved at snowflakes, said, "What do you think?"
The warmth made him giggle, a hearty sight,
"Don't worry, my friends, I'm still feeling bright!"

Echoing Softness

As spring tiptoed near, he felt quite bold,
"I'm a puddle poet, hear my stories told!"
With splashes of laughter, he spun around,
Echoes of chuckles in warm air abound.

His hat began slipping, a glorious sight,
As he told the sun, "You're such a delight!"
His melted dreams sparkled in the sun,
"Embrace this warmth, let's have some fun!"

Light in the Frost

Amidst the chilly breeze, he danced in place,
With a floppy scarf, he embraced his grace.
"No need for sorrow, I'm melting away,"
He shouted with joy, "Let's celebrate the day!"

As puddles formed, he splashed with flair,
"I'm a liquid legend, beyond compare!"
With each drop that fell, his smile grew wide,
"Catch me if you can, I'm winter's pride!"

Echoes of Joy in the Warmth

As the sun shines bright and bold,
The snowman chuckles, feeling old.
With each drip, he starts to grin,
Who knew warmth could feel like a win?

A puddle forms where he once stood,
Swapping snow for a cheerful mood.
His carrot nose begins to droop,
But he dreams of a splashy loop!

Remnants of a Winter's Heart

A frosty friend with a jolly look,
Hoping to leap like a storybook.
But as the rays begin to shine,
He starts wondering, is this divine?

With a wink and a playful sigh,
He waves farewell, but oh, my, my!
A puddle left, but oh, the glee,
For even the melt can be fancy-free!

From Frost to Fusion

Chilly days are fading fast,
Turning memories into a blast.
With a lighthearted wiggle and shake,
Our frosty friend makes quite the break!

No more snowflakes, only splashes,
He dances in puddles, plays with splashes.
A delight, a giggle, what a dash,
Merging mirth with a joyful splash!

When Ice Meets Compassion

In the warmth, he feels the tickle,
Glowing red where the ice starts to trickle.
With a chuckle as drips hit the ground,
He realizes fun knows no bounds!

With each drip and drop, he spins around,
A dancing puddle, joy he has found.
In this thaw, he finds a spark,
Wishing upon the bright sunshine's arc!

Love in the Chill

In the frosty air, we play,
Chasing snowflakes day by day.
A carrot nose, a charming grin,
But warmth creeps in beneath the skin.

Snowball fights erupt with glee,
Giggles hide behind the tree.
We can't resist the sunny rays,
As winter melts in silly ways.

Liquid Memories

A puddle forms where fun was had,
The snowman frowns, his face is sad.
But laughter spills from every crack,
Revealing joy we won't hold back.

As ice melts down like silly goo,
We splash around in vibrant blue.
Each droplet tells a tale or two,
Of frosty days we all once knew.

Snowflakes and Secrets

Whispers float on winter's breath,
Secrets shared till springtime's death.
A chilly hug, a winter waltz,
Until the thaw, we prance and pulse.

Frosty smiles hide warm delights,
Snowball laughter in snowy nights.
The snowman's grin begins to fade,
As playful hearts begin to wade.

Heartbeats in the Frost

With chilly cheeks and playful cheer,
We dance around, embrace the deer.
In frozen fields, we leap and spin,
As heartbeats race with every grin.

The snowman's heart, though cold and white,
Now thumps with joy in the fading light.
A melting smile, a laugh so bright,
Frosty friends, we'll take flight.

Whispering Snowflakes

Snowflakes whisper, dancing light,
They tickle noses, a playful sight.
With frosty giggles, they swirl around,
A winter's jest on frosty ground.

But when the sun gives a cheeky grin,
They start to giggle, letting thin.
A wink from warmth, a teasing dance,
Melting mischief, taken a chance.

Silent Longings

In winter's grasp, a snowman stands,
With a carrot nose and snow-packed hands.
He dreams of spring in silent tones,
While melting puddles moan like stones.

The sun creeps closer, what a tease,
He sighs, 'Oh please, can't you freeze?'
But laughter bubbles with each drip-drop,
As he sways and leans, he can't quite stop.

Melodies Beneath the Melt

Under the sun, a song begins,
With chuckles hidden in icy sins.
The snowman hums with a joyful twist,
Creating chaos from his frosty mist.

Each bead of water sings so sweet,
As puddles form beneath his feet.
"Don't go!" he pleads, with a frosty cheer,
While giggles echo, bringing near.

When Winter Weeps for Spring

Winter pouts with a snowy frown,
As warmth approaches, the snow melts down.
A frosty tear rolls down his cheek,
But laughter bubbles as he is sleek.

He tickles toes with every slide,
A water ballet, oh what a ride!
"Goodbye, my friends!" he gives a shout,
As he dances, there's no doubt.

Heartstrings of Crystal and Flame

A heart of ice with hopes so bright,
Yearns for the sun, a warming light.
With each sunbeam, he starts to sway,
Melting away, in a funny way.

His cheeks turn pink, what a sight to see,
A snowman laughing at his own decree.
With each little drip, he finds delight,
In the silliness of his frosty plight.

Ephemeral Beauty

In winter's chill, he stood so tall,
A cap and scarf, he had it all.
But sunlight danced with a cheeky grin,
And whispered softly, 'Let the fun begin!'

With every ray, he started to fade,
His buttons lost, oh what a charade!
A puddle left where he once posed proud,
He giggled, thinking, 'I'm not allowed!'

The children laughed, they splashed around,
A splashy dance on melting ground.
He chuckled too, in his watery fate,
Finding joy in this silly state.

Melting Moments

Oh, the jolly snowman had a plan,
To catch the sun with a lively tan.
He winked at clouds, 'Let's have some fun!'
But oh, that warmth, he couldn't outrun!

His carrot nose did a little sway,
As he said, 'I'll just melt away!'
The sun chuckled, with rays so bright,
'You'll be a puddle by the night!'

Each drop of water sang a song,
'Why stay frozen when you can belong?'
A dance of joy in a sunny spree,
He laughed, 'Who knew melting felt so free?'

Shards of Light

Amidst the snowflakes, he took a stand,
A frosty fellow in a winter wonderland.
But the sun peeked out with a giggle and glow,
'Hey buddy, it's time for a show!'

His arms outstretched like a silly clown,
In the warm sun, he started to frown.
'I'm not ready for this bright delight!'
But soon he twirled in the golden light.

Each crystal shard began to charm,
As he melted with flair, causing no harm.
With every drip, he felt so spry,
'Who knew melting could make you fly?'

The Warmth Between

In the garden where laughter reigns,
A frosty figure felt the chains.
Those sunny rays wrapped him tight,
As if they said, 'Come dance, take flight!'

His snowy coat began to droop,
But he giggled, joining the troupe.
The kids all cheered, 'Hey look at him!'
As he melted down with a cheeky grin.

Splashes echoed from the nearby brook,
Where he once stood, all it took,
Was a pinch of warmth and a dash of play,
To chase the frost completely away.

Sunlit Reflections

A frosty chap in the sun,
Waves at kids, his icy fun.
But warmth's a sneaky little thief,
Chasing him, beyond belief.

Carrot nose begins to droop,
While giggles form a silly group.
With every ray, his smile droops wide,
As puddles gather by his side.

The children laugh, they give a cheer,
"Hey, look at that! He's shedding year!"
But he just grins, not a care,
A jolly soul in warm sun's stare.

He thinks of summer's lemonade,
And all the fun he's gonna trade.
So let him melt, let him sway,
He'll return on a snowy day!

From Stillness to Flow

Once a solid, still delight,
Now he wiggles, what a sight!
Laughter echoes in the park,
As he turns from snow to spark.

Kids tossing snowballs, dek to deck,
While he's deciding to deck his neck.
With a splash, he starts to dance,
In warm sunshine, he takes his chance.

Melting clumps drip on his feet,
"Oh dear! This is quite a treat!"
Silly grins and giggles ring,
As the seasons start to swing.

Once a statue, now a joke,
But in his heart, the joy still pokes.
"I'll return," he shouts with glee,
"Just you wait and watch, you'll see!"

Whispered Wishes

On a chilly day, he stood tall,
A frosty knight, never small.
But whispers drift through the trees,
"Hey, buddy, feel that warm breeze?"

Down he sank, a soggy best,
While kids laughed, he took the jest.
"I wanted snowball fights today!"
Yet here he melts, oh what a play!

Dreams of cookies, fudge, and cream,
While puddles form, he starts to beam.
With each drip, he laughs and sways,
In the sun's warm, silly rays.

As the sun begins to glow,
He winks, "Goodbye, I'll take it slow."
Bright wishes lift through the air,
He'll return, be tall, and fair!

Trails of Thawing Emotion

In the park, he took a stand,
With frosty fingers, snowball in hand.
Yet giggles rise from here to there,
As sunlight dances in his hair.

Melting jokes and playful schemes,
A snowy soldier, shedding dreams.
"Why's this happening?" he did shout,
While little ones stomped around and clout.

With dribbles drip, and puddles splash,
He wonders why he's in this trash.
Yet laughter swirls, he can't feel sad,
Just silly dances, oh so glad!

So he'll twirl 'til the shadows cast,
Funny stories from the past.
And as he melts, he smiles wide,
For fun will always be his guide!

The Last Breath of Winter's Dance

Frosty gloves wave goodbye,
A clumsy jig on ice does lie.
Stomping feet, a slip, a fall,
Winter's laughter echoes call.

Sunlight peeks with a grin,
Snowflakes twirl, preparing to thin.
Giggles roll as he starts to fade,
In puddles where snowmen once played.

With every thaw, a chuckle's heard,
Melting dreams, an absurd word.
A nose of carrot takes a dive,
As winter's jokes help us survive.

So here's to the snowman, cool and bright,
Waving cheer at the warm sunlight.
He twirls away with snowy glee,
Leaving behind only memories!

Secrets Beneath the Ice

Beneath the frost, oh what a sight,
Laughter lurks in chilly bites.
A secret stash of jokes does lie,
Frozen chuckles in a sly sky.

Melting down, he spills his tales,
Of snowball fights and winter fails.
With each drip, a punchline flows,
As warmth approaches, humor grows.

Carrot noses start to sway,
As warming suns come out to play.
Giggles bounce like snowflakes dance,
Embracing joy, we take a chance.

So lift your glass to winter's jest,
Where every drop brings out the best.
In icy realms, laughter grows,
As secrets bubble up from below!

An Ode to Warmth's Awakening

Oh cozy sun, come out to shine,
Revealing snowmen in a line.
With grins so wide, they take their stand,
In slushy puddles, oh so grand.

Jokes about hats and scarves they share,
As winter's chill begins to wear.
Each drip-drop brings a giggling cheer,
As warmth's embrace draws laughter near.

They wiggle 'round with floppy arms,
Declaring spring's delightful charms.
With melting hearts and silly glee,
These frosty friends are wild and free!

So raise a toast to sunny skies,
Where frozen fun never dies.
In every smirk from winter's end,
Lies a tale we'll always send!

Fragments of a Frozen Dream

In a world of ice, where giggles freeze,
A melting heart brings smiles with ease.
Tiny snowflakes, jokes in flight,
Twist and twirl in pure delight.

Chunks of snow with purpose tease,
As winter's warmth begins to please.
A splash of white, a twinkling eye,
Reflects the laughter soaring high.

With every drip, a story told,
Of icy mishaps, brave and bold.
Fragments lost, but spirits stay,
Making silly memories in the fray.

So gather 'round, don't let it pass,
For melting dreams can always last.
In every drop that falls apart,
Lies the echo of a joyful heart!

Frosty Souls in Thawing Light

In the sun, we stand and sway,
Grinning wide, we melt away.
A carrot nose, it droops and frowns,
Puddle smiles in quirky towns.

Laughter comes from every side,
As snowflakes try to run and hide.
A dancing hat upon our head,
Wishing snow to stay instead.

The sun comes out, a teasing friend,
With warmth that makes us bend and blend.
We play along, no cause for strife,
Just frosty souls embracing life.

Chills of a Tender Embrace

A gentle hug, but it's a tease,
With all this warmth, I feel a breeze.
My frozen heart, it starts to sway,
In giggles of the sunny play.

The snowman's grin grows wider still,
As icy bits begin to spill.
A sloshy dance around his feet,
In puddles where the cold ones meet.

A wink from sun, a snowy jest,
Why can't we stay? We are the best!
Yet in this moment, joy will last,
Even as the cold slips past.

Icy Veins, Warm Wishes

In winter's chill, we laughed aloud,
With frozen dreams beneath a shroud.
But hear the sun, it calls our names,
Transforming us into poolside games.

With icy veins, we're feeling bold,
Little wishes start to unfold.
A splash here, a giggle there,
As we toss snowballs into the air.

Though noses drip, and hats go flop,
We'll savor each jump, spin, and hop.
A melting day we won't regret,
With frosty fun, our hearts won't fret.

A Heart of Frost Unraveled

Once a figure, proud and tall,
Now a puddle, having a ball.
With every drop, a cheer erupts,
As chilly charm just warms us up.

A frosty heart begins to tease,
While giggling chills bring us to knees.
We'd play accordion in the glow,
With twinkling eyes, embracing slow.

So let me drip, a silly sight,
In every drop, pure joy takes flight.
Embracing warmth, we dance anew,
As frosty tales become the view.

Surrendering to Spring

A frosty fellow with a top hat,
Stands tall but whispers, "Where's my mat?"
The sunlight beams, in laughter it plays,
As snowflakes giggle and drift away.

He shakes his fist at the sun above,
"You sneak! You thief! You dare to move?"
With puddles forming, he starts to fret,
But he can't resist the warm vignette.

The birds are chirping, the flowers bloom,
His icy heart begins to feel the gloom.
"Oh, winter's end is quite absurd!"
He tries to fend off spring's sweet word.

With every drip and splutter, he sighs,
It's hard to look cool in melting guise.
His carrot nose begins to sag,
"Guess I'm just a soggy old rag!"

Chasing the Last Flake

In a world of snow, he reigns as king,
With every flake, he dances and swings.
"One more flake! Don't slip away!"
He tumbles over, what a dismay!

He lunges past a sunbeam's glare,
"Not yet! I swear it's still fair!"
But warmth descends like an eager friend,
His icy reign comes to an end.

He leaps and hops like a bunny's dare,
"Where are you, flakes? Come show me care!"
But slowly they giggle, lost in the bright,
Chasing the last flake feels quite the plight.

As he melts near a patch of grass,
He shouts, "Winter, don't let this pass!"
But the sun just winks, with a mischievous glow,
"Time for some fun, my frosty amigo!"

The Warmest Goodbye

Old Jack Frost with a tearful wink,
Waves farewell as he starts to sink.
"Goodbye my friends, the chill has fled,"
As dew drops tease and buds turn red.

He grabs a scarf, says, "Take that sun!"
But melting giggles have already begun.
Rivers of water laugh and flow,
"Don't be sad, it's time to go!"

The sun's warm smiles wrap 'round his toes,
While he shivers, shaking off his clothes.
"I wanted snowball fights and frigid nights,"
But here I am, in spring's bright lights.

With one last sigh, he waves his hand,
"It's really not bad in the sunny land!"
He may be gone, but don't you fret,
For joyful memories linger yet.

Frostbitten Heartstrings

A frosty heart, so proud and bold,
With tears of ice, a story told.
"I'm melting, screaming! I'm falling apart!"
Caught in a tussle with a warm-hearted tart.

He watched as friends slid down a hill,
Floating on snow, giving him a thrill.
But warmth whispered sweet, "Join in the fun!"
His icy facade was coming undone.

He pulled at his hat, gave it a tug,
"Hold tight to dreams, just one more hug!"
But the sun played tricks with a grin so wide,
As his heartstrings thawed, he couldn't hide.

He let out a laugh, began to dance,
With puddles splashing at every chance.
Though frostbitten feelings fade with the days,
He learned that joy comes in melting rays.

Portrait of a Thaw

In winter's grip, he stood so proud,
With carrot nose and scarf, a crowd.
But sunbeams danced, a cheeky spree,
And said, 'Hey mate, come swim with me!'

His top hat drooped in the warm light,
His button eyes lost their delight.
He waved goodbye to flurries white,
And soaked in sun, a funny sight!

His arms of sticks began to droop,
A puddle formed—oh what a goop!
With giggles loud, he slid away,
To join the ducks in a splish-splash play!

As he departed, puddles rolled,
His frosty tales now wet and bold.
He chuckled soft, 'This isn't bad,
More fun than being cold and sad!'

A Melted Photograph

Captured in a frame of ice,
His smile warm, oh so precise.
But warmth seeped in to spoil the fun,
And he began to come undone!

His chin dripped slowly down his chest,
He tried to hold, but none could rest.
An icicle winked, 'Don't be so vain,
Let's hop in puddles, it's not in vain!'

The backdrop blurred, a water dance,
He squeaked and slipped, oh what a chance!
A photo now, smeared memories,
Of laughter shared and sunny breeze.

Now he's a smear on grandma's wall,
Yet still he smiles, he's having a ball.
For every drop and dribble dear,
He knows there's fun in every tear!

Hope Under Ice

Beneath the frost, a heartbeat sings,
A playful jingle in winter's rings.
With every thaw, his dreams take flight,
To dance with daisies in the light.

He chuckled low, 'I'm not the end,
When spring arrives, I'll still transcend.'
Though drips and drops may start to show,
His laughter echoes, a warm glow.

The squirrels skitter, the sun peeks in,
He shimmies softly, a silly grin.
For in the warmth, he finds his wits,
Plotting snowball fights and sunny sits.

So let him melt, let nature tease,
He'll sprout some joy with every breeze.
For even ice can find a way,
To laugh and play on a bright day!

Emblems of Change

With each thawed patch, a giggle grows,
Under cheery skies where laughter flows.
A snowy hat begins to flop,
And puddles gather, a sloshy hop!

His arms of twig start to let go,
In splashes bright, he steals the show.
A mighty wipe, a snowball flies,
From melting hands to gleeful cries!

Every drip tells a story new,
Of funny fables and skies so blue.
"I'm not so sad," he tried to declare,
"Just like other seasons, life's fair!"

The frosty days turn into dreams,
With joy that blooms in sunny beams.
For change is just a twist of fate,
And laughter echoes—it's never too late!

Love's Embrace in Winter's End

In the chill of winter's air,
A snowman dreams without a care.
His buttons shiny, eyes so bright,
He winks at sun, 'Let's start a fight!'

But as the daytime brings warm cheer,
He starts to lose his pointy spear.
His carrot nose begins to droop,
'Why's the sun such a sneaky troupe?'

With each ray that starts to shine,
His hope melts down like chocolate wine.
'Oh no!' he cries, 'What's this I see?
It's lemonade, not meant for me!'

Yet as he shuffles into spring,
New friends appear, and joy they bring.
Though puddles form, he takes a chance,
And joins the kids in a silly dance.

The Fragile Thaw of Winter's Grasp

Underneath a robin's song,
A snowman wonders, 'What went wrong?'
His top hat's tilted, oh so wrong,
He giggles on, singing along.

The sun shows up, grinning wide,
And the snowman starts to slide.
'Is that my hat I see, all wet?
Oh no! I'll be a big regret!'

His icy heart begins to sway,
As winter's grasp starts to decay.
'Please, dear sun, don't melt me fast,
I want to party, not be past!'

But friends are here, they grab his hand,
And they dance like they had planned.
Though puddles form, they laugh and shout,
'Oh, winter's end, let's turn about!'

Lament of the Frosted Heart

In frosty nights with moon's bright beam,
A jolly snowman starts to dream.
'Will summer come and steal my luck?
Oh no, old friend! Don't lose that puck!'

His smile melts, he sighs so deep,
'Oh what a fate, this snowman creep!'
The sun looks down, with rays so bold,
'Just wait! There's ice cream to be sold!'

He waves to kids who skate and play,
But worries whisper, 'They'll go away.'
'Don't let them toss my hat around,
I'll stand my ground on chilly ground!'

Winter's warmth begins to spread,
As laughter fills the day instead.
With one last scoop, he feels the joy,
A melting heart, a playful boy.

Frosted Dreams

In a world where snowflakes fall,
A snowman stands, two feet so tall.
His dreams are frosted, bright as day,
'Will someone come to laugh and play?'

As day breaks forth, the sun does beam,
He feels the warmth, like a sweet dream.
'Oh please, don't let my smile decay,
I'd rather melt in a fun ballet!'

With kiddie shouts and snowball fights,
He twirls and giggles, what a sight!
Though puddles form, he does not care,
'Let's dance together, without a scare!'

And as he slips, he chuckles loud,
With every fall, he feels so proud.
Winter's song may fade away,
But frosted dreams will always stay.

Reflections in a Puddle

In the park he stood so proud,
A hat too big, it looked quite loud.
Snowballs fought with laughter and cheer,
But now he sweats—the end is near.

With each sunbeam, he starts to sway,
His carrot nose begins to stray.
Birds fly by with cheeky grins,
And all the snowflakes shout, "No wins!"

A puddle forms, his feet get wet,
A slippery jive, a slow regret.
He wobbles left, then right, oh dear!
What's this? A duck? Now that's unclear!

Down he goes with a comedic splash,
A watery dance, a frosty crash.
Reflecting smiles, he winks with glee,
"Next time, a sunhat will suit me!"

From Frost to Flow

Once so icy, firm, and bold,
Now he's melting, truth be told.
With every laugh from kids nearby,
He tips his hat and starts to cry.

A slip and slide, he does a twirl,
A happy leap—what a swirl!
His scarf now drips, a soggy mess,
The weather's won, he'll confess!

"Oh dear, did I just lose a foot?
This chilly body's starting to shoot!
But hey, look at my shiny flair,
I'm a water feature—what a rare!"

As puddles gather, kids take a dive,
A splashing game, oh how they thrive!
He chuckles soft, amidst the play,
"Can a snowman have a splashy day?"

The Slow Fade of Winter

In the garden, he did pose,
A sight of fun, with sparkling nose.
The sun creeps in, a warming tease,
And with a sigh, he starts to freeze.

What's that? A sunbeam on his hat!
He laughs aloud, then plops down flat.
With each tick-tock, he turns to mush,
A giggly grin—he's in a rush!

"Goodbye to frost, hello to green!
This drip's the best that I have seen!
Rolling around like a water blob,
A laugh, a splash, freeze your job!"

Now little kids, they take a chance,
A splashy splash, a silly dance.
He quips, "What fun, men made of snow,
Can vanish quick—just watch me go!"

Awakened by Sunshine

He stood quite still, at dawn's first light,
With eyes so bright, a silly sight.
But as the sun gave him a wink,
His body shivered, lost in ink.

"Is that a bird, or just my nose?
I swear I felt it wiggle—who knows?"
A slip on ice, he takes a bow,
"Guess I'm not so solid now!"

Children giggle, chasing him near,
With each warm ray, they cheer and cheer.
"Embrace the melt; don't fight the fun,
Now I'm a splishy-splash! Oh run!"

As puddles blossom in morning's gaze,
He revels in his watery phase.
"Why fret my friends? Here's the best part—
Free lemonade from a melting heart!"

Whispers of Winter

Frosty friend, oh what a sight,
With a carrot nose, you're quite polite.
Chasing snowflakes and dodging the sun,
You giggle and melt, oh what fun!

Children build you, with laughter and cheer,
Yet the sun's warm rays bring a hint of fear.
"Don't leave me," you shout, as puddles appear,
But who can resist a warm mug of beer?

Snowballs fly, and you just can't hide,
As buckets of warmth slip right inside.
You flinch and you quiver, with a frosty frown,
While everyone giggles at your wintery crown.

So dance in the breeze, oh comical sprite,
Embrace the meltdown, it's a funny sight.
With a wink and a grin, you'll make your depart,
A puddle of joy and a joyful heart.

The Warmth Beneath

Oh chilly fellow, standing so stout,
Your icy grin gives you clout.
The sun is shining; oh where do you go?
Into a puddle, your fate is a show.

Laughter erupts as you shrink away,
A splash by the kids, it's a sunny play.
"Help me!" you cry, but they giggle with glee,
A puddle of snowman, what a sight to see!

The warmth laughs loud, as you slowly drip,
Down to the ground, you take quite a trip.
"Can I borrow a hat?" you jokingly plea,
But all that you get is a chuckle, wee hee!

So cheer up, dear friend, it's not the end,
You'll still be a part of the tales that we send.
As winter departs, just remember the fun,
For even a snowman can bask in the sun.

Icicles and Ember

Icicles dangling, a sparkling show,
While you wobble and sway, it seems quite a show.
Hats fly off with a poke and a tease,
Who knew warmth could turn you to cheese?

With a giggle, you melt, like ice cream on cake,
"Wait, don't leave yet!" you start to shake.
Furious flurries attempt to assist,
But sip after sip, the fun starts to twist.

A cup of hot cocoa, a marshmallow dance,
You slip and slide in a snowy romance.
As friends give a cheer with their cups raised high,
They toast your demise—oh my, oh my!

So dance in delight, with laughter so bright,
As embers glow warm, you'll fade out of sight.
From ice to a puddle, you'll frolic away,
With memories of fun, on this sunny day.

A Thawing Tale

Once a frosty giant of fluff and delight,
You stood in the yard, a glorious sight.
But as sunshine peeked and the temperatures rose,
Your giggles grew faint, as the laughter froze.

Your carrot nose twitched at the merest bright ray,
"Can I borrow some warmth?" you comically say.
But a child threw a snowball, and giggle rang out,
Soon you were dancing, while melting about.

With each little drip, the fun kept on flow,
You made a big splash, oh the joy we bestow!
"Chill out!" cried the kids, with glee in their tone,
As you jiggled and wobbled, a thawing cyclone.

So raise up a cheer for the fuzzy and wet,
A snowman's demise is a tale we won't forget.
The laughter extends, as the sun lights the way,
For even in melting, there's fun in a day.

Gentle Hues of Change

A frosty face starts to pout,
As the sun peeks, what's this about?
A sleigh full of joy, but he's in a bind,
With puddles forming, oh dear, never mind!

His carrot nose droops in despair,
While kids run around, without a care.
"Don't melt away, just have some fun,
It's only warm weather and not a gun!"

His scarf slips down, a floppy mess,
He trips on snowballs just to impress.
But laughter echoes, a giggle spree,
"Let's have a dance, just you and me!"

Oh, joy of spring, it's poking through,
With all his friends, they're on a zoo.
At last he smiles, a silly grin,
For melting isn't the end, but a win!

A Whispering Sun

A sunbeam tickles his frosty toes,
With laughter ringing, he starts to pose.
Droplets dance like they own the floor,
"Hey, look at me, I'm a slip 'n' score!"

His friends all cheer, "Come join the fun!"
As he slides down hills, oh, what a run!
They giggle and tease, give him a shove,
Now slippery chaos is what they love!

A cup of cocoa, and he gets a taste,
"Is this fondue or can I go to waste?"
With cream atop, it's quite a treat,
He sweeps it up with frosty feet!

Yet just as he thinks he's found his groove,
A puddle forms and starts to move.
But with a wink, he waves goodbye,
"Catch me later in the sky!"

Radiance Breaking Through

A wobbly walk in the sunny glow,
Melting joy he simply can't forgo.
His eyes twinkle bright, like stars at night,
With giggles that burst, oh what a sight!

Friends shout, "Hey, dance with us some more!"
He spins and slips, starts a snowball war!
But who knew laughter could cause such heat?
His icy heart skips its frosty beat!

He joins the chase, with a silly hat,
But down he goes, and lands—splat!
"Pure snow joy, what's a little drip?"
With each little splash, he does a flip!

A melting song, the wind does sing,
As warm days tease, a funny fling.
In every drop, there's joy anew,
Dancing in colors, his spirit grew!

Silent Sorrows

In the glow of bright, he feels dismay,
With frosty chills starting to sway.
"Why must I fade when I'm having fun?"
The clouds giggle softly, "It's just begun!"

The children laugh, play games so sweet,
While he watches with droopy feet.
"Throw one more snowball before I go,
Let's make a mess, let's start a show!"

His heart feels heavy, though he tries to cheer,
He cracks a smile with a hint of fear.
"Goodbye, dear friends, I'll melt but stay,
In every laugh, I'll find my way!"

As he drips away, he adds to the cheer,
In every puddle, his laughter's near.
A silly goodbye, with a wink and a wave,
For melting isn't the end, it's a brave!